The Return of Crazy Horse

The Return of
Crazy Horse

WILLIAM KOTZWINKLE
illustrated by JOE SERVELLO

Frog, Ltd.
Berkeley, California

Published by Frog, Ltd.

Frog, Ltd. books are distributed by
North Atlantic Books
P.O. Box 12327
Berkeley, California 94712

Cover design by Paula Morrison
Book design by Jennifer Dunn

North Atlantic Books are available through most bookstores. To contact North Atlantic directly, call 800-337-2665 or visit our website at www.northatlanticbooks.com.

Substantial discounts on bulk quantities of North Atlantic books are available to corporations, professional associations, and other organizations. For details and discount information, contact the special sales department at North Atlantic Books.

Library of Congress Cataloging-in-Publication Data

Kotzwinkle, William.
     The return of Crazy Horse / by William Kotzwinkle.
          p. cm.
        ISBN 1-58394-047-2 (alk. paper)
        1. Crazy Horse, ca. 1842-1877—Juvenile literature. 2. Crazy Horse, ca. 1842-1877—Portraits—Juvenile literature. 3. Oglala Indians—Portraits—Juvenile literature. 4. Ziolkowski, Korczak, 1908—Juvenile literature. 5. Crazy Horse Mountain (S.D.)—History—Juvenile literature. [1. Crazy Horse, ca. 1842-1877. 2. Oglala Indians—Biography. 3. Indians of North America—Great Plains—Biography. 4. Crazy Horse Mountain (S.D.)—History.] I. Title.

E99.03 K6 2001
730'.92—dc21
                                                                        2001018965

The mountain dreamed in the sun.

On the plains below, the Sioux Indians roamed.
Chief among them was the mighty warrior Crazy Horse.

Led by Crazy Horse and other great Chiefs,
the Sioux fought the white soldiers for many years,
and won.

They defeated General Custer's army
at the Battle of Little Big Horn.

But the Sioux were defeated in the end,
losing their men and their land,
and the mountain slept on.

"Where are your lands now, Crazy Horse?"
asked a victorious white soldier.
"Where my dead lie buried."

Crazy Horse went to Soldier's Town to talk peace.
The white men said he could talk to their Chief.

Instead, they led him to a prison.
When he saw barred windows, he tried to escape,
  and the soldiers bayoneted him to death.

Years   and   years

         went by.

All the soldiers of that war, except for a few old Indians,
passed away;   and the mountain slept on—
    for the time of a mountain is not the time of men.

Nearby, another mountain in the range began to take on
a strange face—of a famous man,
    a great white Chief, George Washington.

Soon the face of Thomas Jefferson appeared beside it,
and Theodore Roosevelt, and Abraham Lincoln,
all great leaders of the United States.

Still the mountain dreamed,
   its own face shapeless.

One day it felt a rumbling inside itself.
Then the mountain learned it was not just a mountain
but a great Chief too.

It heard this from a man named Korczak Ziolkowski.

He, and Chief Henry Standing Bear, an old Sioux Indian,
saw Chief Crazy Horse in the mountain.

Now he is returning. He is riding out of the mountain.
The shape of his fierce head is slowly forming,
and his arm is pointing out of the shapeless rock.

Chief Crazy Horse is being helped out by
Korczak Ziolkowski, who talks to the mountain
with a great roar of dynamite.

The day is filled with explosive words.

It is not easy to be friends with a mountain.

The mountain is stubborn,
    but it has met a man who is just as stubborn.

He is bringing Crazy Horse out,
    pulling him, pushing him,
        blasting him free of his cold stone veil.

The mountain listens, and obeys.
Within, Crazy Horse speaks,
      urging his horse forward, out of the cloud of rock.

Outside, Ziolkowski rides his own horse,
a great steel horse that pushes rock down the mountainside,
clearing a path for the Chief.

There is the scream of a shuddering drill,
which only a strong man can hold, which makes a man deaf,
makes his spine rattle and his skeleton dance.

Ziolkowski hangs onto this demon drill,
  chiseling across the face of Crazy Horse with it,
muttering at the stone to come loose, to let Crazy Horse free.

The Chief's ride is slow, for it is a mountain ride.

It will take many years to be done.

We will be growing old,

but the mountain will still be young,
　　and from it will come Crazy Horse, riding to the sun.

Dance, Crazy Horse,
gallop from the invisible hunting ground,
into the sun.

KORCZAK ZIOLKOWSKI began blasting the stone of Thunderhead Mountain in the Black Hills of South Dakota into his statue of Crazy Horse in June 3, 1948. He labored thirty-four years on the mountain, to the very last day of his life. His great work is continued by his wife, Ruth, and their children— Casimir, Monique, Jadwiga, Dawn, Adam, Anne, and Mark. Upon completion, it will be the largest sculpture on earth, taller than the Great Pyramid of Egypt.

WILLIAM KOTZWINKLE is the author of the enduring children's classic, *E.T. The Extraterrestrial*. He is a two-time winner of the National Magazine Award For Fiction, and of the World Fantasy Award. He has supported Native American educational activities for many years, and picked herbs with a Mohawk medicine man.

Crazy Horse always wore a stone beside his ear.
When questioned about it by his people, his answer was,

"I will return to you in the stone."

To visit the Crazy Horse Memorial:
In South Dakota take Interstate 90 to the Rapid City Exit. Take Highway 16/385 South to Mt. Rushmore. Crazy Horse is seventeen miles from Mt. Rushmore. Signs mark the way.

JOE SERVELLO has illustrated over sixty books, many of them for William Kotzwinkle, including their best-selling *Trouble In Bugland*. He has been a professional actor, and an art and drama teacher. His historic murals fill the walls of his hometown of Altoona, Pa.